How can you make it move?

Steve, Amy, Jo, and Zack are playing in the park with Zack's truck. Zack gets in first, and the others help him to get moving.

A kick from behind works, too. Look at the truck go!

Not too hard! You might break it.

3

So pushes and pulls start things moving. A kick does, too. It's like a hard push.

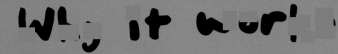

Everything needs a push or a pull to make it start moving. Pushes and pulls are called forces. A push is a force that makes things move away from you.

A kick is a sort of push. A pull is also a force, but it moves things toward you. What pushes and pulls are there when you swim, play tennis, or ride a bike?

Solve the puzzle!

Why is Zack worried about kicking the truck? Take a paper cup and see what pushes, pulls, and kicks can do to its shape.

5

What makes a swing change direction?

At the playground, Jo gets on the tire. Steve gives her a push to make her swing. Zack also wants to give her a push, but the tire is going in the wrong direction.

Can we make Jo swing over to Zack?

I think a push from the side will make Jo change direction.

6

7

Let's see how the children find out.

8

3

Pushes can also make it swing in a circle.

But a push on only one side makes it spin around and around.

Why it works

When something is moving in a straight line, a push or a pull from the side makes it change direction. Pushes and pulls can also make things spin or move in a circle. Think about a soccer ball. You can kick it in a straight line, and then you can make it change direction with another kick. You can also make it spin by twisting it with your hand.

4

Solve the puzzle

How can a puppy make you walk in circles? Think about what happens if you have a puppy on a leash and it wants to go in a different direction.

9

How do you make a merry-go-round speed up?

The children run to play on the merry-go-round. Steve and Amy get on and Zack gives them a push.

11

Let's see how the children find out.

12

If I push it the other way, it slows down, then turns the other way. Look!

So a bigger push must make a merry-go-round spin faster, too. But a push in the opposite direction makes it slow down and stop.

3

A push or a pull makes things start to move. An extra push or pull in the same direction makes them go faster. Pushing things harder also makes them go faster. So pushing a merry-go-round harder makes it spin faster. But a push or pull in the opposite direction makes things slow down and go the other way.

Solve the puzzle

Are things easier to push when they get heavier? Try adding wooden blocks to a toy truck one at a time. Does it get easier or harder to push? **13**

Why don't you slide up a slide?

The children line up to go on the slide. Amy goes first. She climbs up the steps, then sits down at the top. When she lets go, Amy whizzes down to the bottom of the slide.

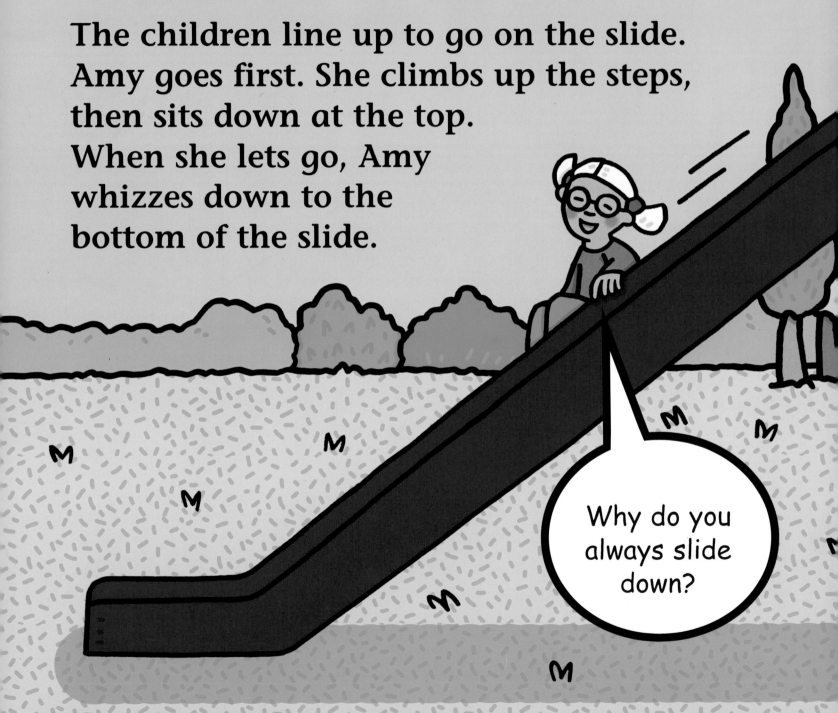

Why do you always slide down?

When I let go from the top of the ramp, the car goes faster.

3

It's going farther, too. The longer slope must mean the force is pulling the car for longer.

Why it works

When you sit on a slide, you slide down. If you throw a ball into the air, it falls to the ground. These things happen because of a force that pulls everything down to the ground. We call this force gravity. You can't see it, but gravity is pulling down on you all the time. Without it, we would float around like astronauts in space.

Solve th puzzle

Do heavy things fall faster? Make two balls of modeling clay, one twice as big as the other. Drop them from the same height at the same time. Which one hits the ground first?

7.

Why does a kite fly?

The wind starts to blow, so the children play with Steve's kite. Zack lets go of the kite and it flies up into the air. Steve holds onto the string so it doesn't fly away.

Why does a kite fly? I can't see anything pushing it.

It must be the wind pushing against the kite. I have to hold on tight.

Let's see how the children find out.

3

I can also make my pinwheel spin by blowing on it.

So moving air can push things and make them move, even though you can't see it.

How it works

Wind is moving air. Though you can't see it, it can push against things. On a windy day, you can feel the wind pushing against you when you walk along, and you can often see it blowing leaves along the ground. The same force pushes a kite up into the sky and makes a pinwheel spin around and around.

Solve the puzzle!

Can moving water push things? Think about waves on a beach or squirting something with a hose.

21

Did you solve the puzzles?

Why is Zack worried about kicking the truck?

Pushes and pulls make things move, but they can also make things change shape or break. A hard push like a kick can squash or dent a paper cup. Pushing and pulling can twist and bend it. A hard pull can also tear things.

How can a puppy make you walk in circles?

A young dog on a leash doesn't always want to go the same direction as you want to go. It can pull you around and around, making it hard to walk in a straight line! Sometimes the wind can blow you in a different direction, too.

22

Are heavier things easier to push?

The heavier something gets, the harder it is to push. When you add blocks to the truck, it needs a harder push to make it move. When a heavy thing is moving, it is also harder to stop.

Do things fall faster if they are heavier?

No. If you let go of the big and small balls of clay at the same time, they will hit the ground together. What happens when you drop them both from higher up?

Can moving water push things?

Yes. Moving water can push with a strong force. If someone squirts you with a hose, you can feel the force of the water. A big wave on a beach can easily knock you over. Before there were engines, people used the force of water to drive machines. Water from a river pushed on the paddles of a big waterwheel and made it spin around.

23

Index

© Aladdin Books Ltd 2002
10 9 8 7 6 5 4 3 2 1

Designed and produced by
Aladdin Books Ltd
28 Percy Street
London W1T 2BZ

First published in
the United States in 2002 by
Copper Beech Books,
an imprint of
The Millbrook Press
2 Old New Milford Road
Brookfield, Connecticut 06804

ISBN 0-7613-2822-X (Library bdg.)
ISBN 0-7613-1838-0 (Paper ed.)

Cataloging-in-Publication data is
on file at the Library of Congress.

Printed in U.A.E.
All rights reserved

Literacy Consultant
Jackie Holderness
Westminster Institute of Education
Oxford Brookes University, England

Science Consultants
Helen Wilson and David Coates
Westminster Institute of Education
Oxford Brookes University, England

Science Tester
Alex Laar

Design
Flick, Book Design and Graphics

Illustration
Jo Moore